HOW TO BE THE BEST GRANDPARENT EVER

Essential Tips, Fun Activities, and Heartfelt Advice to Create Unforgettable Memories and Strong Bonds

By Michael Summers

INTRODUCTION

"Grandparents are the bridge between yesterday's wisdom and tomorrow's dreams, teaching love that transcends generations."

There is no joy quite like that of becoming a grandparent. The moment you hold your grandchild for the first time, something profound and indescribable happens. It's a love that feels both familiar and brand new, a second chance to experience the magic of childhood—only this time, without the sleepless nights and the constant worry that comes with being a parent. Grandparenting is a privilege, an opportunity to create a bond that is unique, beautiful, and enduring. It's a role filled with love, wisdom, and, most importantly, presence. But as the world changes, so too does the way we approach this cherished role.

Gone are the days when grandparents were merely occasional visitors, bringing sweets and stories from the past. Today, grandparents play a more active and influential role in their grandchildren's lives than ever before. Families are evolving, and so are the expectations placed on grandparents. Some are full-time caregivers, stepping in to help raise their grandkids while parents juggle demanding careers. Others are long-distance grandparents, relying on technology to bridge the miles and maintain a strong connection. And then there are those who are simply there as a pillar of emotional support, providing the wisdom and warmth that only a grandparent can offer.

Regardless of the circumstances, one thing remains the same: grandparents matter. More than just a source of nostalgia or an occasional treat-giver, they are role models, confidants, and storytellers. They provide a sense of continuity, anchoring children in their family history while guiding them toward the future. In many ways, grandparents are the keepers of family traditions, the quiet observers who watch over generations, imparting lessons not just through words but through the way they live their lives. And yet, stepping into this role can sometimes feel daunting. Parenting styles have shifted, new technologies shape the way children communicate, and the world is vastly different from the one in which you raised your own kids.

Understanding today's parenting landscape is crucial to being an effective and supportive grandparent. Parents today are navigating a fast-paced world filled with pressures that previous generations never faced. The rise of digital technology means that children are growing up with screens, social media, and constant connectivity, while parents are expected to balance work, home life, and an ever-changing set of societal expectations. Gentle parenting, positive discipline, and child-led learning are just a few of the modern philosophies shaping today's families, and while these approaches may differ from the methods you were familiar with, they come from the same place of love and care. One of the greatest gifts a grandparent can give is understanding—respecting the parenting choices of their children while offering wisdom without judgment.

This book is here to help you navigate this incredible journey. Whether you are a hands-on grandparent who spends every afternoon with your grandkids, or someone who connects through video calls and holiday visits, this book will provide you with insights, advice, and inspiration to make the most of your role. Throughout these pages, you'll discover ways to build meaningful connections with your grandchildren, engage in activities that create lasting memories, and adapt to the changes that come with modern grandparenting. You'll learn how to balance your wisdom with respect for parents' boundaries, how to offer guidance without overstepping, and how to navigate the joys and challenges of being a grandparent in today's world.

Beyond practical tips, this book is also a celebration of the incredible bond between grandparents and grandchildren. It's about the laughter shared over bedtime stories, the secret handshakes, the whispered conversations that hold more meaning than any grand declaration. It's about the way a grandparent's love lingers long after childhood, shaping a grandchild's sense of self, their values, and their understanding of unconditional love. Through real-life stories, heartfelt reflections, and hands-on strategies, this book will empower you to embrace your role with confidence and joy.

Grandparenting is a journey, one that evolves as your grandchildren grow. It is not about being perfect or following a set script—it is about being present, being engaged, and being the kind of grandparent your grandchildren will cherish. Whether you are sharing your family's history, teaching them life skills, or simply offering a warm hug at the right moment, know that you are making a difference. You are shaping their world in ways both big and small, and that, more than anything, is what makes being a grandparent so extraordinary.

So, take a deep breath, embrace the adventure, and let's embark on this journey together. There is so much to discover, so many moments to savor, and a lifetime of love to share. Welcome to the incredible world of grandparenting.

Chapter 1

The Magic of Being a Grandparent

There is something truly extraordinary about stepping into the role of a grandparent. It is a transformation that brings forth an entirely new perspective on love, family, and the passage of time. Becoming a grandparent is not just about welcoming a new member into the family; it is about rediscovering the beauty of childhood through fresh eyes, relishing in the small joys that might have been overlooked during the busy years of parenting. It is a chance to be present, to be a source of love, laughter, and wisdom without the weight of primary responsibility. This is the magic of grandparenting—the ability to shape lives in ways that are both gentle and profound, creating bonds that last a lifetime.

What makes grandparents so special? It is not just the treats they slip into little hands or the bedtime stories they tell with a twinkle in their eye. It is the deep and unwavering sense of security they provide. Grandparents are a source of unconditional love, a steady presence in a child's life that exists outside of the daily ups and downs of parental discipline and expectations. They have the freedom to be a listening ear, a reassuring voice, and a safe haven in a world that can sometimes feel overwhelming to young minds. This special role allows grandparents to nurture a child's self-esteem, helping them feel valued and supported in a way that is distinct from the role of a parent.

The emotional and psychological benefits for grandchildren who have a strong relationship with their grandparents are immeasurable. Studies have shown that children who maintain close relationships with their grandparents tend to have higher emotional intelligence, a greater sense of security, and stronger family values. Grandparents provide children with a historical context of their roots, helping them feel connected to something greater than themselves. They serve as living history books, sharing family stories and traditions that might otherwise be lost with time. These connections offer children a foundation of belonging, which in turn fosters confidence and resilience.

Beyond emotional support, grandparents also offer perspective. They have lived through different eras, experienced challenges and triumphs, and learned invaluable lessons along the way. Because they are often removed from the day-to-day responsibilities of raising children, they can offer guidance with patience and wisdom that is not clouded by exhaustion or stress. They can help children navigate difficulties, whether it is handling school pressures, overcoming fears, or developing a sense of self-worth. The gentle, guiding hand of a grandparent can provide children with a sense of stability and perspective that enriches their development in meaningful ways.

One of the most remarkable aspects of grandparenting is the contrast between parenting and this new role. Parenting is a job that comes with an intense sense of responsibility—ensuring that children are well-fed, educated, disciplined, and cared for at every moment. It can be exhausting, filled with worries and obligations that sometimes make it difficult to simply enjoy the moments as they come. Grandparenting, however, is a second chance at experiencing childhood's wonder without the daily stress of discipline and structure. While parents may be focused on the practicalities of raising a child, grandparents can embrace a more relaxed and joyful presence, offering fun, wisdom, and encouragement without the weight of making all the tough decisions.

This distinction does not mean that grandparents do not play a critical role in child development. In fact, it is their ability to provide love and mentorship without the daily pressures of parenthood that makes them so essential. Their role is one of support, encouragement, and joy. Grandparents can be the ones who say, "Yes, let's build that fort," or "Of course, let's bake cookies before dinner," providing a kind of spontaneity and indulgence that children treasure. This does not mean undermining parents or disregarding their rules, but rather complementing their efforts with an added layer of affection and playfulness.

The magic of being a grandparent is best illustrated in the countless stories of those who have left an indelible mark on their grandchildren's lives. Take, for instance, the grandmother who taught her grandson to garden, not realizing that those afternoons spent digging in the soil would inspire a lifelong love for nature. Or the grandfather who spent years teaching his granddaughter how to play chess, an activity that not only strengthened their bond but also built her confidence and strategic thinking skills. These stories are not just heartwarming; they are powerful reminders of the immense influence that grandparents wield, often in the most unexpected ways.

Even in moments of hardship, grandparents have the ability to bring comfort and hope. Many children who face difficulties, such as a divorce in the family or struggles at school, find solace in their grandparents' presence. The simple act of being there, of offering a hug, a listening ear, or a reassuring word, can make all the difference in a child's ability to process emotions and find strength in adversity. Grandparents, with their life experience and patient hearts, can serve as beacons of stability in times of uncertainty.

The beauty of grandparenting lies in the simplicity of moments shared. It is in the way a child's face lights up when they see their grandparent waiting for them after school. It is in the bedtime stories that turn into cherished memories, the inside jokes that no one else understands, and the traditions that continue through generations. These are the things that children carry with them into adulthood—the laughter, the love, and the profound knowledge that they were deeply cherished.

In embracing the magic of being a grandparent, there is a wonderful opportunity to reflect on one's own childhood and the influences that shaped it. Whether a person had strong relationships with their own grandparents or not, becoming one presents a chance to create something truly special. It is a role filled with possibility, one that can bring immense joy not only to the grandchild but also to the grandparent themselves. The love shared in this relationship is one of life's greatest treasures, and the legacy left behind is one that will be felt for generations to come.

As we explore the many facets of grandparenting in this book, we will delve deeper into the ways in which grandparents can nurture, guide, and support their grandchildren in meaningful ways. From the practicalities of building strong relationships to the challenges of navigating modern family dynamics, this journey will celebrate all that it means to be a grandparent in today's world. But above all, it will serve as a reminder that being a grandparent is a gift—one that comes with boundless love, endless wonder, and the potential to make a lasting difference in the life of a child.

Chapter 2

Building a Strong and Meaningful Bond

The relationship between a grandparent and grandchild is a unique and precious connection, one that has the potential to be deeply fulfilling for both. Unlike parents, who bear the daily responsibilities of discipline and routine, grandparents can focus on the sheer joy of nurturing a bond that is built on love, trust, and an unwavering sense of support. This connection, however, does not happen automatically. It requires effort, creativity, and most importantly, presence. It is about stepping into a child's world in a way that feels natural, engaging, and, at times, wonderfully silly.

Connecting with grandchildren of all ages means understanding that each stage of life comes with its own set of challenges and delights. Babies and toddlers are easy—let's face it, they think you're a rock star simply for making funny faces and handing them a spoon to bang on a pot. A three-year-old will listen with rapt attention as you tell them for the hundredth time about the "old days" when phones had cords and cartoons only aired on Saturday mornings. School-age children, however, require a different approach. They are curious, full of energy, and often eager to share their latest discoveries, whether it's a newfound ability to ride a bike or an obsession with dinosaurs. Showing genuine interest in their world, whether it means learning the names of all 150 Pokémon or sitting through an animated movie you don't understand, is a surefire way to remain relevant and fun in their eyes.

Then, of course, come the teenagers. Ah, the teenage years—a phase where a simple text message from you might be met with an eye-roll, and an attempt at a heartfelt conversation may be answered with one-word responses. But don't be discouraged. The beauty of grandparenting is that you're in the unique position of being able to offer unconditional love without the daily nagging that often comes with parenting. Teenagers might not always admit it, but they need you. They need your wisdom, your perspective, and—believe it or not—your approval. A well-timed comment about how cool their taste in music is or how impressive their latest accomplishment may be can do wonders. And if you're willing to let them teach you how to use the latest social media trend (even if you don't care about TikTok), you've just earned yourself some major grandparent points.

One of the most beautiful ways to build a meaningful bond is by establishing traditions that are just between you and your grandchild. These don't have to be elaborate or expensive, just consistent. Maybe it's a secret handshake that only the two of you know. Maybe it's a monthly ice cream outing where calories don't count. Perhaps it's a bedtime story that you read over the phone if you live far away. Whatever it is, it should be something that becomes a cherished part of their lives, a little ritual that says, "This is ours."

Rituals are powerful because they provide children with a sense of stability and something to look forward to. Weekly calls, bedtime stories, special outings—these seemingly small acts are what create lifelong memories. When a grandchild grows up and looks back, it won't be the extravagant gifts that stand out, but the comfort of knowing that every Sunday afternoon, Grandma or Grandpa would call to chat about their week. It will be the memory of knowing that no matter what, there was always a warm hug waiting, always a reassuring voice on the other end of the line.

Being a grandparent also means being a safe space. Life is not always easy for children, and sometimes, they need someone who will simply listen without judgment. They need to know that, in a world filled with expectations and rules, there is one person who will love them exactly as they are. This doesn't mean undermining parents or allowing misbehavior, but it does mean providing a place where emotions are welcomed and understood. A child who knows they can confide in their grandparent about their fears, their dreams, or even just the rough day they had at school, is a child who feels secure in their place in the world.

A sense of humor goes a long way in strengthening the grandparent-grandchild bond. Life is serious enough; being able to laugh together builds an emotional connection that is unbreakable. So, don't be afraid to be silly. Wear the funny hat, do the ridiculous dance, attempt the latest slang (even if it embarrasses them). Laughter is one of the most powerful ways to create memories that last a lifetime. When your grandchild thinks of you, let them remember the joy, the fun, the warmth, and the moments when the world felt just a little bit lighter.

Practical ways to deepen this bond also include engaging in their favorite hobbies and interests. If your grandchild loves sports, attend their games and cheer them on like the world's most enthusiastic fan. If they enjoy arts and crafts, join them in creating something together, whether it's painting a picture or building a birdhouse. For book lovers, start a two-person book club where you read the same book and discuss it together. Technology can be a bridge rather than a barrier; playing online games together or sending voice messages with silly jokes can keep the connection strong even across distances.

Another powerful way to forge an unbreakable bond is through storytelling. Share tales of your childhood, let them laugh at the idea of a world without the internet, and tell them about the lessons you've learned along the way. Children love hearing about the "old days," and these stories help them understand not just where they come from, but who they are. If possible, keep a journal filled with memories, advice, and funny anecdotes to pass down to them one day—a tangible reminder of your love.

Building a strong bond with your grandchildren doesn't require grand gestures or endless wisdom. It simply requires love, attention, and a willingness to meet them where they are. Be their biggest cheerleader, their safe space, and their partner in fun. Whether they are five or fifteen, they will carry that love with them always, and in turn, they will pass it down to future generations. That is the true magic of being a grandparent.

Chapter 3

Communication and Respecting the Parents' Role

One of the most delicate aspects of being a grandparent is learning how to navigate the relationship with both your grandchildren and their parents. The excitement of grandparenting often comes with an urge to share wisdom, give advice, and even step in when things don't seem to be going as expected. However, this well-intended involvement can sometimes be perceived as interference, creating unnecessary tension. The key to a harmonious relationship lies in finding a balance—being a source of support without overstepping boundaries, offering guidance without criticism, and fostering open and respectful communication with both parents and grandchildren.

Supporting without overstepping is a fine art. It requires the ability to offer help in a way that is welcome rather than imposed. Parents today face a barrage of information, from parenting books to social media advice, and they are often trying to carve their own path in raising their children. As a grandparent, the best approach is to be available rather than directive. Instead of saying, "You should do this," try, "When you were little, we tried this, and it seemed to work well. Would you like to hear about it?" Framing advice as a shared experience rather than an instruction makes it more likely to be well received. And if the parents decline the advice? Respect their decision with grace. Remember, your role is to support, not to dictate.

Advice is a tricky thing. No one wants to feel judged, and yet, as a grandparent, it can be difficult to hold back when you see a situation that reminds you of your own parenting days. The key is to offer advice in a way that doesn't sound critical. Rather than pointing out what you think is wrong, emphasize what is working. Compliment the parents on what they are doing well before gently suggesting an alternative approach. Saying something like, "I love how patient you are with bedtime—when you were little, I found a little lullaby helped too," makes a world of difference compared to, "They'll never sleep if you keep doing it that way." Encouragement fosters trust; criticism creates distance.

Family conflicts are inevitable. Generations bring different viewpoints, and sometimes, misunderstandings arise. The secret to resolving family conflicts peacefully is to prioritize the relationship over the need to be right. If disagreements occur, take a step back and evaluate whether this is truly a battle worth fighting. Will your concern still be relevant a year from now? If not, it may be best to let it go. And if it is, address it with kindness. Phrases such as, "I see how much you care about this, and I respect that. Can we talk about a compromise?" open the door for productive discussions rather than escalating tensions. When conflicts do arise, lead with love, practice patience, and remind yourself that the most important thing is preserving the family bond.

Building a strong relationship with your grandchild's parents is just as important as nurturing the relationship with your grandchild. Parents are the gatekeepers to your access to their children, and a warm, respectful relationship with them paves the way for a strong bond with your grandkids. Expressing appreciation for their efforts, respecting their rules, and seeking ways to support them rather than question them will strengthen your relationship. A simple, "You're doing an amazing job," can go a long way in reinforcing a positive dynamic.

There are many ways to show respect for parenting choices while maintaining a strong presence in your grandchild's life. For example, if the parents have set rules about screen time, make an effort to follow those guidelines even if you might personally have a different perspective. If they prefer a particular diet for their child, respect their wishes rather than sneaking in forbidden treats. These small gestures signal that you support their parenting approach, making them more likely to trust you with their children.

Humor can also be a powerful tool in navigating the grandparent-parent relationship. When tensions arise, a well-timed joke or lighthearted comment can diffuse potential conflict. If your grandchild is covered in stickers from head to toe and their parents are exasperated, a simple, "Well, at least they have a strong sense of self-expression!" can break the tension and bring laughter into the room. Finding ways to lighten the moment shows that you are on the parents' side and can create a bridge between generations.

In real-life situations, navigating these dynamics takes practice. Take the case of Susan, a grandmother who found herself disagreeing with her daughter about discipline. Rather than arguing, Susan chose to observe and understand her daughter's parenting style before offering any advice. Over time, she built trust by reinforcing the positive aspects of her daughter's approach and only gently suggesting ideas when asked. This helped maintain a loving relationship without friction. Then there's Mark, a grandfather who was eager to share his love of woodworking with his grandson, but the parents were concerned about safety. Instead of pushing back, Mark collaborated with them to create a safe and supervised way for his grandson to participate. These small but meaningful adjustments make all the difference in keeping the family unit strong.

At the heart of grandparenting is the understanding that your role has shifted. You are no longer the primary caregiver; instead, you have stepped into the role of mentor, friend, and source of unconditional love. Embracing this new role with respect for boundaries, patience in offering guidance, and a deep well of love for both parents and grandchildren will create a foundation of trust that benefits the entire family. By fostering a spirit of collaboration rather than control, you not only strengthen your own relationship with your grandkids but also contribute to a family dynamic built on love, respect, and joy.

Every grandparent wants to be a valued part of their grandchild's life. The best way to ensure that happens is to create an atmosphere of understanding, laughter, and appreciation within the entire family. With patience, open-mindedness, and a touch of humor, you can enjoy a fulfilling and lasting bond with your grandchildren while maintaining a respectful and loving relationship with their parents. After all, a family that laughs together, grows together.

Chapter 4

The Art of Being Present

Being a grandparent is one of life's greatest joys, but the true magic lies not just in the title, but in the time spent together. The art of being present is a skill that requires conscious effort in today's fast-paced world, where distractions are endless, and schedules are often packed. Grandparenting is an opportunity to slow things down and savor the moments that matter most, making time for your grandkids in ways that enrich both your lives.

Making time for your grandchildren doesn't always mean setting aside entire days or planning grand excursions. It's about quality over quantity, being fully engaged in the time you do spend together. Whether it's a five-minute video call to hear about their day, a handwritten note slipped into their backpack, or a short visit to their soccer game, these seemingly small acts add up to a lifetime of cherished memories. Kids may not always remember the expensive gifts you gave them, but they will always remember how you made them feel.

One-on-one time is where the deepest connections are formed. While group gatherings with the whole family are wonderful, carving out moments where it's just you and your grandchild creates a special intimacy. Whether it's taking a quiet walk together, cooking their favorite meal, or simply lying on the grass looking up at the clouds, these moments of uninterrupted presence speak volumes. They tell your grandchild: "You are important to me. I love spending time with just you." It's in these moments that grandchildren open up the most, sharing their hopes, their worries, and their dreams in a way they might not in a crowded room.

Mindful grandparenting is about tuning in, not just being physically present but truly paying attention. It means putting the phone away, turning off the TV, and focusing on the person in front of you. Kids have an incredible way of knowing when they are being half-listened to, and they will always remember if you were fully there for them. Instead of answering messages while they talk, look into their eyes. Instead of absentmindedly nodding while they tell you about their latest school project, ask thoughtful questions that show you care. Being fully present in these moments not only deepens your bond but also teaches them the invaluable lesson of being present for others.

Some of the most impactful gestures are the smallest ones. A wink across the dinner table when they make a funny joke, a gentle squeeze of the hand when they're nervous about something, or a handwritten letter just because—these are the things that stay with a child long into adulthood. Grandparents have the power to make a child feel seen, heard, and valued in a way that lasts a lifetime. It's the little traditions, the inside jokes, the way you always have their favorite snack ready when they visit—these are the building blocks of a strong and meaningful relationship.

Humor, too, plays an important role in being present. Life is full of serious moments, and children thrive when they are reminded that laughter is just as important as responsibility. Don't be afraid to be silly—put on a funny hat, dance around the living room, attempt their latest slang (even if you butcher it). Being playful breaks down walls and creates a bond that is rooted in joy. It shows them that no matter how old you are, there is always room for fun.

For example, consider a grandmother who made it a tradition to teach her granddaughter a "word of the day" in a different language every time they spoke. This simple, lighthearted ritual turned into a treasured bond, where the granddaughter would eagerly call to learn her new word and practice it all week. Or the grandfather who made up bedtime stories starring his grandchild as the hero, a tradition that continued well into their teenage years as a cherished reminder of their special connection.

Being present also means understanding and respecting the individual personality of each grandchild. One might love to sit and talk for hours, while another prefers engaging in a hands-on project. Adapting your time together to fit their preferences shows them that you see and appreciate them for who they truly are. If one grandchild is fascinated by space, take them to a planetarium or read books about astronauts together. If another loves baking, spend an afternoon making cookies and letting them take the lead. These seemingly small acts create powerful memories and reinforce a child's sense of belonging and confidence.

Another aspect of being fully present is recognizing that as children grow, their needs and ways of connecting change. A toddler might cling to you with excitement every time you visit, while a teenager might seem distant or more engaged in their own world. This doesn't mean your relationship is fading—it simply means it's evolving. Find creative ways to stay connected with older grandchildren, such as texting them a funny meme, watching a movie they love together, or even just asking for their opinions on things that matter to them. Showing genuine interest in their evolving lives fosters a deep and lasting bond.

At the end of the day, the best way to be present is to simply show up—physically, emotionally, and wholeheartedly. Be there for the big moments, but also the small ones. Listen with an open heart, laugh freely, and embrace the wonderful opportunity to be part of their lives in a way that is meaningful and lasting. Being present isn't just about the time you give; it's about the love, attention, and joy that fill that time. And that is what your grandchildren will remember most.

Chapter 5

Fun and Engaging Activities for Every Age

Spending time with your grandchildren should be filled with laughter, curiosity, and the simple joys of discovery. Whether they are just learning to walk or navigating their teenage years, every moment together presents an opportunity to bond, learn, and create lasting memories. The key to making the most of these moments is tailoring activities to their age, interests, and personality, ensuring that time spent together is both meaningful and fun.

For the youngest grandchildren, those between the ages of 0-3, sensory play is a wonderful way to engage with their natural curiosity. Simple activities such as playing with textured fabrics, making homemade playdough, or filling a tub with water and letting them splash are more than just play—they are opportunities for learning and bonding. Storytelling at this stage is especially powerful. Even if they don't understand all the words, they respond to the rhythm of your voice, the warmth of your presence, and the excitement in your storytelling. Reading books with engaging pictures, singing nursery rhymes, or simply narrating your actions as you go about the day builds a strong emotional connection and lays the foundation for a lifelong love of learning. A fun idea is to create a "story bag" filled with objects that relate to different stories—pull one out, and let the object inspire a new tale together.

As children grow into the 4-7 age range, their imaginations expand, and their desire for hands-on experiences grows. This is a golden period for arts and crafts, where creativity knows no bounds. Making simple collages from magazine cutouts, finger painting, or even building castles out of cardboard boxes can lead to hours of enjoyment. Outdoor games become even more exciting, whether it's playing hopscotch, going on a nature scavenger hunt, or simply running through a sprinkler on a warm day. Simple science experiments, like mixing baking soda with vinegar to make a "volcano," add an extra layer of excitement and education. The joy in their eyes when they witness something "magical" happening is priceless. Consider planting a small garden together, teaching them about nature as they water and care for their plants. Watching something grow over time can be an incredible lesson in patience and responsibility.

For grandchildren between 8-12 years old, this is the perfect time to introduce them to new skills and mini-adventures. They love challenges and independence but still cherish the guidance of a grandparent. Teaching them how to cook a simple dish, playing strategic board games together, or embarking on a "treasure hunt" around the neighborhood can make your time together truly special. These years are also a fantastic time to bond over shared hobbies. If they love photography, let them borrow a camera and explore. If they're into sports, join them for a friendly competition. This is also a great time to take them on small outings—perhaps a fishing trip, a visit to a historical site, or an afternoon spent at a local library picking out books together. The memories created in these shared adventures will stay with them for a lifetime.

Another great activity for this age group is creating a family time capsule. Gather small items that represent their current interests, write letters to their future selves, and seal everything in a container to be opened years later. This kind of activity not only strengthens your bond but also teaches them about the importance of memory and reflection.

Teenagers, often thought to be more independent and less interested in spending time with their grandparents, actually appreciate meaningful interactions more than they let on. The trick is to respect their growing independence while finding creative ways to stay connected. Instead of expecting them to engage in traditional "kid" activities, meet them where they are. If they love technology, ask them to show you how to use a new app or play a video game together. If they're into music, ask for recommendations and genuinely listen. Respecting their individuality and offering a space for conversation without judgment can turn your relationship into one of mentorship and trust. Sharing life wisdom in small doses, rather than through long lectures, will also help. A simple, "When I was your age, I went through something similar," can open the door to meaningful conversations.

Another great way to bond with teenagers is through shared projects. Perhaps you can work on a DIY home improvement task together, build a birdhouse, or even start a small business venture like selling homemade crafts online. Grandparents have a wealth of experience, and passing down knowledge about responsibility, creativity, and problem-solving can be both fun and educational. Travel is another fantastic way to bond—whether it's a short road trip or a weekend getaway, seeing new places together can foster unforgettable memories and rich conversations about the world.

No matter the age, the power of shared laughter cannot be underestimated. Telling funny stories from your past, joking around, and being willing to be a little silly can break down walls and bring you closer together. Children and teens alike love seeing their grandparents as real people, full of humor and warmth, rather than just authority figures from another generation.

The most important takeaway is that you don't need grand gestures or elaborate plans to create meaningful experiences. It's the little things— spending time, listening, being engaged, and showing genuine interest—that truly matter. Whether it's rolling a ball back and forth with a toddler, baking cookies with a 6-year-old, teaching a 10-year-old how to play chess, or simply texting a teenager to check in, every interaction strengthens your bond. And at the end of the day, those are the moments that both you and your grandkids will treasure forever.

Chapter 6

Storytelling and Passing Down Family History

Stories are the thread that connects generations, weaving a rich tapestry of memories, lessons, and traditions. Every family has a history filled with triumphs, challenges, humorous moments, and love that deserves to be preserved and shared. As a grandparent, you have the unique privilege of being the storyteller, the keeper of wisdom, and the bridge between past and future. The power of storytelling is not just about entertaining—it's about anchoring grandchildren to their roots, helping them understand where they come from, and fostering a deep sense of belonging.

One of the most magical things about storytelling is that it allows children to experience a time they never lived in. Through your stories, they can imagine the world as it was decades ago—before smartphones, social media, and instant gratification. Share with them tales of your childhood, the games you played, the mischief you got into, and the lessons you learned. Tell them about their great-grandparents, how they met, the traditions they cherished, and how the world was different back then. Children love knowing that their family is part of something bigger, that they belong to a long line of people who have laughed, loved, and overcome challenges just as they will.

Beyond spoken words, storytelling can take many forms. One beautiful way to preserve family history is by creating a family tree together. Sit down with your grandchildren and sketch out a visual representation of their lineage. As you do, tell stories about each ancestor—where they lived, what they did, and what made them special. If you have old photographs, even better! Show them pictures of their great-great-grandparents, explaining their lives and experiences. This not only strengthens their sense of identity but also creates a tangible connection to their heritage.

Another meaningful way to pass down stories is by starting a grandparent-grandchild journal. This could be a shared notebook where both of you write back and forth, sharing thoughts, reflections, or little notes about your days. Perhaps you write a childhood memory one day, and your grandchild writes about their favorite school experience the next. Over time, this journal becomes a priceless keepsake, filled with memories, advice, and love that can be cherished for years to come.

Writing letters for your grandchildren to open in the future is another heartfelt tradition. Imagine them discovering a letter from you on their wedding day, on their first day of college, or when they become a parent themselves. These letters can be filled with words of encouragement, wisdom, and reflections on life. Write to them about what makes them special, the values you hope they carry forward, and the dreams you have for them. These letters become treasures, a tangible reminder of your love that they can hold onto long after childhood fades into adulthood.

Humor plays a crucial role in storytelling. Not every family story has to be profound or dramatic —sometimes, the most memorable tales are the funny ones. Share the time you got caught sneaking cookies from the kitchen, the embarrassing moment at a family gathering, or the hilarious misunderstandings that turned into cherished inside jokes. Laughter creates bonds, and when grandchildren hear these stories, they see you not just as a grandparent, but as a person who has lived, stumbled, and laughed just like they do.

Storytelling isn't just about preserving the past—it's also about creating new stories in the present. Make it a habit to tell bedtime stories that blend imagination with personal experiences. Take turns adding to a story together, letting creativity flow freely. If you have a family recipe that has been passed down through generations, turn cooking into an opportunity to share its history. Tell them how their great-grandmother used to make that same dish, how it brought the family together, and how each bite is a piece of history they are carrying forward.

At its core, storytelling and passing down family history is about connection. It's about letting your grandchildren know that they are part of something bigger, that they come from a lineage of resilience, love, and adventure. It's about giving them the gift of belonging, the wisdom of experience, and the comfort of knowing that no matter what, they are always surrounded by the stories and love of those who came before them. And in doing so, you ensure that your family's legacy lives on—not just in history, but in hearts.

Chapter 7

The Grandparent as a Teacher and Mentor

Being a grandparent is more than just sharing love and providing comfort—it is also an opportunity to be a teacher and a mentor. With years of experience, wisdom, and patience, grandparents are in a unique position to pass down life skills, offer guidance, and instill values that shape a grandchild's journey. Teaching isn't just about sitting down with a lesson plan—it happens in everyday moments, in the stories told, in the hands-on experiences shared, and in the quiet moments of encouragement.

One of the most rewarding ways to teach is through life skills—those little things that children and even young adults will carry with them for the rest of their lives. Cooking together is a wonderful way to bond while passing down cherished family recipes. There is something magical about flour-dusted hands, the scent of warm cookies in the oven, and the laughter that fills the kitchen. Teaching a grandchild to prepare a meal isn't just about food—it's about tradition, patience, and the simple joy of creating something with your hands. And of course, there's always the added benefit of getting to eat the results—unless, of course, they get a little too experimental with the spices. A particularly fun twist is hosting "cooking competitions" where you and your grandchild each prepare a small dish and let the rest of the family vote on the best creation.

Gardening is another life skill that offers lessons beyond just growing plants. Whether it's teaching them how to plant a seed, pull weeds, or care for flowers, gardening instills patience, responsibility, and an appreciation for nature. And if they get muddy in the process? Even better! Those are the kind of memories that stick—mud-covered hands and faces full of excitement when they see the first green shoots poke through the soil. Gardening also teaches valuable lessons about nurturing and persistence. Just as a garden requires consistent care, love, and patience, so do relationships and personal growth. You might even create a "Grandparent's Garden" together, where each grandchild gets to plant and tend to something of their own.

Budgeting is a skill that many people only learn later in life, often through trial and error. Grandparents can help their grandkids understand the value of money early on, whether it's through simple lessons like saving allowances, understanding the difference between needs and wants, or even setting up a small lemonade stand together to teach basic business principles. Watching a child's face light up when they realize they've saved enough for something special is a lesson in patience and responsibility that will serve them well in adulthood. You might even introduce them to a piggy bank challenge, where they set a financial goal and track their savings over time, learning firsthand about the rewards of discipline and perseverance.

Beyond practical skills, grandparents also have the unique ability to nurture a love for learning. Helping with homework isn't just about solving math problems—it's about showing a child that learning is a journey, not just a task. Reading together, taking trips to the library, or even making a game out of learning can transform something "boring" into an adventure. Science experiments in the kitchen, crossword puzzles to expand vocabulary, or simply asking open-ended questions that encourage curiosity can make a world of difference in a child's perception of education. If you have expertise in a particular subject, whether it's history, art, or mechanics, sharing your knowledge in an engaging way makes the learning process much more enriching and fun.

Supporting a grandchild's passions and interests is another way to be an effective mentor. Whether they are interested in painting, sports, music, or technology, showing enthusiasm for what they love fosters confidence and motivation. Attending their performances, cheering them on at games, or even just listening as they explain their latest project goes a long way in making them feel valued. Grandparents have the unique ability to be a safe space—offering encouragement without pressure, support without expectation. A particularly impactful approach is introducing them to new experiences they might not otherwise explore. Maybe a grandchild who loves drawing would enjoy a visit to an art museum, or a science-loving grandchild might be fascinated by a trip to a planetarium.

Teaching social skills and manners in a fun way is another invaluable role grandparents can play. A child might not listen to their parents when they say, "Say please and thank you," but when

Grandpa makes a silly game out of it or Grandma offers a fun reward, suddenly, etiquette becomes exciting. Using role-playing games to practice ordering food at a restaurant, writing thank-you notes together, or demonstrating the importance of kindness and empathy through storytelling all contribute to shaping a child's character in an engaging and memorable way. Grandparents can also introduce "random acts of kindness" as a regular activity—whether it's baking cookies for a neighbor, leaving positive notes for classmates, or volunteering together at a local shelter. These small gestures reinforce empathy and gratitude in ways that will stick with them for life.

The key to mentoring as a grandparent is to make it lighthearted, engaging, and full of love. Children learn best when they don't feel like they are being lectured but instead feel like they are part of an exciting journey. Humor can go a long way—whether it's laughing at a failed recipe attempt, sharing a childhood story where you made a hilarious mistake, or poking fun at yourself when you mispronounce the latest slang. The goal isn't perfection—it's connection. Even mistakes become lessons when shared with warmth and humor. If a baking project goes terribly wrong, turning it into a funny memory instead of a disaster teaches resilience and adaptability in a way no formal lesson ever could.

As grandchildren grow, the lessons they learn from their grandparents become the foundation for their own adult lives. The skills, wisdom, and kindness shared today will echo into the future, shaping the way they navigate the world, interact with others, and carry forward the traditions that were lovingly passed down to them. Being a grandparent is an opportunity not just to love, but to guide, to teach, and to leave a legacy of knowledge, patience, and joy. Every lesson, every shared moment, becomes a lasting thread in the fabric of their lives—one they will look back on with appreciation and, hopefully, a smile.

Chapter 8

Long-Distance Grandparenting: Staying Connected Across Miles

Being a grandparent from a distance may not be what you envisioned, but it can still be an incredibly meaningful and fulfilling role. While you may not have the luxury of spontaneous visits or daily in-person interactions, there are countless ways to bridge the gap and maintain a strong, loving connection with your grandchildren. In today's digital age, technology has opened doors that previous generations never had, allowing grandparents to be present in their grandchildren's lives in new and creative ways.

One of the most effective ways to stay engaged is through video calls, but let's face it—kids can have short attention spans. The trick is to make these calls fun and interactive. Instead of just asking the usual, "How was school?" try having themed calls. Maybe one day you both wear silly hats, or another time you each bring a mystery object to show and tell. You could read a book together, play a guessing game, or even have a virtual tea party. Grandparents who add a touch of creativity to their calls will find that their grandkids look forward to them rather than seeing them as a chore. And remember, even a quick five-minute check-in can make a huge difference.

Beyond video calls, one of the most cherished ways to stay connected is through good old-fashioned letters and care packages. There is something magical about receiving a letter in the mail, especially in an era where handwritten notes are becoming rare. Send postcards from your hometown, include funny doodles, or even write a short story featuring your grandchild as the hero. And let's not forget the joy of care packages—perhaps a box filled with their favorite snacks, a small toy, or a craft project you can do together over the phone. These tangible reminders of your love can turn an ordinary day into something special.

Another wonderful way to stay connected is by creating a virtual storytime tradition. Whether through live video chats or pre-recorded videos, reading books to your grandkids is a simple yet powerful way to nurture your bond. Choose books that match their interests, use funny voices, and engage them by asking questions about the story. If they're old enough, you can even take turns reading to each other. This tradition not only builds a love for storytelling but also creates a comforting routine they will look forward to. To make it even more interactive, consider reading books with a series element so they eagerly await the next chapter with you.

For the tech-savvy grandparent, online games and interactive activities can be a fantastic way to engage with grandchildren. Whether it's playing a multiplayer video game together, solving puzzles on an app, or competing in online trivia, these activities provide a fun and engaging way to spend time together. If your grandchild loves to draw, try using a digital drawing app where you can collaborate on artwork in real time. For older grandchildren, watching a favorite show together and discussing it afterward can create a shared experience despite the miles between you. You might even start a "movie club," where you watch the same film separately and then discuss it on a call, turning it into your special bonding time.

Another great idea is to create a joint project that you both contribute to over time. This could be a scrapbook that each of you adds to and mails back and forth, a shared Google document where you write a story together, or even a virtual garden where you plan and discuss plant care. A collaborative project gives you both something to look forward to and ensures you always have a meaningful reason to reach out.

Of course, while virtual connections are wonderful, nothing quite replaces in-person visits. When the opportunity arises, planning meaningful visits is key. Rather than cramming every moment with activities, focus on quality over quantity. Perhaps there's a tradition you can create, like making breakfast together every morning or having a "Grandparent's Adventure Day" where they get to choose the itinerary. The key is to be present and make the most of the time you have together, ensuring that each visit leaves behind memories to cherish until the next one.

Planning for visits also means setting up special activities that celebrate your unique relationship. You might start a tradition where you always bake a certain treat together, take a picture in the same location each time, or leave a small keepsake for them to find after you leave. These small, intentional moments help create a sense of continuity between visits, reinforcing your bond even when you're apart.

It's also important to acknowledge the emotions that come with being a long-distance grandparent. Missing milestones, birthdays, and everyday moments can be difficult, and it's okay to feel sad about the distance. However, rather than dwelling on what's missing, focus on what you can do to strengthen your connection. Express your love often, in as many ways as possible, and find joy in the small but meaningful interactions that bridge the miles.

Long-distance grandparenting requires creativity, effort, and a little bit of humor. While you may not be there for every little moment, the love and connection you build will last a lifetime. Grandchildren don't measure love by proximity— they measure it by presence, by effort, and by the warmth they feel whenever they hear your voice or read your words. So embrace the adventure, find new ways to connect, and never underestimate the power of a grandparent's love, no matter the miles between you.

Chapter 9

When Life Gets Tough: Supporting Your Grandkids Through Challenges

Life is not always sunshine and laughter, and as much as we'd love to shield our grandchildren from hardship, challenges are an inevitable part of growing up. Whether they are navigating family struggles, heartbreaks, academic difficulties, or mental health concerns, having a grandparent as a steady and loving presence can make all the difference. The beauty of grandparenting lies in the ability to provide unwavering support, a nonjudgmental listening ear, and wisdom born from life's own ups and downs.

One of the toughest things a child can go through is family turmoil—whether it's divorce, a big move, or tension between parents. While parents may be wrapped up in the logistics of these transitions, grandparents have the unique ability to provide emotional refuge. A phone call, a visit, or even a simple letter reminding them they are loved can be an anchor in uncertain times. Sometimes, just having someone who listens without judgment is enough to soothe their worries. Grandparents can also offer perspective: "When I was young, I went through something similar. It was hard, but I got through it, and you will too." Sharing stories of resilience helps them feel less alone and gives them hope that things will get better.

Heartbreak is another challenge that, while universal, can feel overwhelming in the moment. Whether it's the loss of a friendship, a first romantic breakup, or the disappointment of not making a sports team, these moments can feel like the end of the world to a child or teenager. This is where a grandparent's perspective and gentle humor can work wonders. Instead of dismissing their feelings, acknowledge them: "I know this hurts right now, and that's okay. But I promise, one day you'll look back and see that this was just a stepping stone to something better." And if the occasion calls for it, don't be afraid to offer a bit of lighthearted wisdom—maybe even an amusing tale about your own embarrassing heartbreak to show them that life moves on, and laughter is never far behind.

Struggles at school—whether academic or social—can take a toll on a grandchild's confidence. Perhaps they're falling behind in math, struggling to make friends, or feeling lost in a sea of expectations. Grandparents can step in as a source of encouragement, providing reassurance without pressure. If schoolwork is the issue, learning together in a no-pressure environment can be a game-changer. Turning lessons into fun challenges, helping with homework over video calls, or sharing tricks that helped you when you were younger can make all the difference. And when social struggles arise, being a cheerleader from the sidelines—reminding them of their worth, teaching them the value of kindness, and reinforcing the idea that friendships come and go—can help them navigate these challenges with more confidence.

Mental health and emotional well-being are topics that are thankfully becoming more openly discussed, but they still require careful attention. If your grandchild is showing signs of anxiety, sadness, or withdrawal, your support can be a lifeline. Encouraging open conversations about feelings, making sure they know it's okay to talk about their emotions, and validating their experiences are powerful ways to be there for them. If needed, gently encouraging parents to seek professional help while offering your own unconditional love can be the balance they need. Remind them, "You are not alone. No matter what, I am here for you." Sometimes, just hearing those words is enough to bring comfort.

A particularly powerful way to support a grandchild is through consistency and routine. Life's toughest moments often feel less daunting when there's a steady presence to rely on. Consider setting up weekly check-in calls, scheduling special one-on-one outings, or even maintaining a tradition, like sending postcards with encouraging messages. These small gestures can serve as comforting reminders that no matter what's happening, they have someone in their corner.

Beyond just listening, helping your grandchild build resilience is one of the greatest gifts you can offer. Teach them coping strategies like journaling, deep breathing, or engaging in a creative outlet. Encourage them to set small goals and celebrate their progress, no matter how minor. If they fail at something, help them reframe it as a learning experience rather than a defeat. Share stories of your own setbacks and triumphs to show them that perseverance leads to growth.

When offering advice, be mindful of the balance between wisdom and space. Sometimes, children and teenagers need to vent without immediately being given a solution. Instead of jumping in with fixes, ask them, "Would you like my advice, or do you just want me to listen?" Giving them autonomy in how they receive support fosters trust and makes them more likely to open up to you in the future.

The most powerful thing a grandparent can offer during tough times is consistency. Being a steady, unwavering source of love, encouragement, and wisdom provides security in a world that often feels chaotic. Whether it's through phone calls, visits, handwritten letters, or even silly traditions that make them smile, the effort you put into staying present in their lives will have a lasting impact. Your presence is a reminder that they are never alone, that they are loved beyond measure, and that no challenge is too big when faced with the support of family.

In the end, life's hardships shape us, but it's love that carries us through. As a grandparent, your role isn't to fix every problem, but to walk alongside your grandchild through it all, offering kindness, perspective, and unwavering support. And if all else fails, a batch of homemade cookies and a warm hug never hurt anyone. More often than not, it's the little things—the small reassurances, the quiet moments of laughter, and the unwavering presence—that make the biggest difference in a grandchild's heart.

Chapter 10

Grandparenting in the Digital Age

The world has changed in ways many of us never imagined. There was a time when family news arrived in handwritten letters, kids played outside until the streetlights came on, and "screen time" meant watching Saturday morning cartoons. But today, our grandchildren are growing up in a world where social media, smartphones, and virtual connections are the norm. It can feel overwhelming at times, trying to keep up with all these new ways of communicating and connecting. However, rather than resisting these changes, embracing them can open up new and wonderful ways to stay involved in your grandchild's life.

Understanding social media and online safety is an important first step in navigating this digital world alongside your grandkids. While you may not be interested in posting selfies or following the latest online trends, having a basic grasp of platforms like Instagram, TikTok, and Snapchat allows you to engage in conversations about their digital lives.

Ask your grandchild to give you a "tour" of their favorite apps—it's a great way to bond while learning about the platforms they spend so much time on. Plus, it's a surefire way to impress them. There's nothing quite like the look on a teenager's face when their grandparent correctly uses the word "meme."

That being said, the online world is not all fun and games. Cyberbullying, privacy concerns, and unrealistic social media comparisons are real issues that can impact a child's well-being. While parents take the lead in setting digital boundaries, grandparents can play an important role as trusted confidants. A simple, "You can always talk to me if something online ever makes you feel uncomfortable," can open the door for conversations they might hesitate to have with their parents. And if your grandchild ever rolls their eyes at you for warning them about internet safety, remind them that you're from the generation that survived rotary phones and party lines—so you know a thing or two about privacy concerns!

Technology also presents an incredible opportunity for grandparents to stay connected with grandkids, especially when distance is a factor. Video calls, instant messaging, and even sharing funny memes or GIFs can keep the relationship alive in a way that feels natural to them. Instead of the usual "How was your day?" calls, try making video chats more interactive. Read a book together, play an online game, or watch the same show and discuss it. Some tech-savvy grandparents even send daily "Grandma or Grandpa Challenges," like "Tell me the funniest thing that happened at school today!"—turning digital communication into something fun and meaningful.

Of course, while embracing technology is wonderful, it doesn't mean abandoning the traditions that make grandparenting special. Finding the right balance between modern trends and old-fashioned wisdom is key. Maybe your grandchild loves texting, but you also send them handwritten letters every so often to remind them of the charm of receiving mail. Maybe they enjoy online games, but you also introduce them to classic board games during visits. Blending the best of both worlds ensures that while they grow up surrounded by screens, they also appreciate the value of unplugged moments and face-to-face connections.

Grandparents also have a unique opportunity to bridge generational gaps by sharing personal experiences in ways that feel relevant to today's world. A teenager struggling with self-esteem due to social media comparisons might find comfort in hearing about the pressures you faced in your youth. A child fascinated by technology might love hearing about the "cutting-edge" gadgets of your time, like cassette tapes and dial-up internet. By tying past experiences to modern challenges, you create a common ground where lessons from one era still hold meaning in another.

Embracing change while staying true to your values is perhaps the greatest balancing act of all. You don't have to change who you are to connect with your grandchildren—you simply have to be open to meeting them where they are. Whether it's learning to send emojis, watching their favorite YouTuber, or even making a silly TikTok dance video together (don't worry, they'll guide you through it), the willingness to engage in their world speaks volumes. At the same time, sharing your own passions—whether it's storytelling, cooking, or music—gives them insight into where they come from and what truly matters.

At the heart of it all, grandparenting in the digital age is still about the same thing it has always been: love, connection, and presence. Whether through a screen, a letter, or a long embrace during a visit, what truly matters is that your grandchild knows they are valued, supported, and deeply loved. Technology may change, trends may evolve, but the role of a grandparent as a source of wisdom, laughter, and unwavering support remains timeless.

Chapter 11

Grandparenting in Blended and Multicultural Families

Family today looks different than it did generations ago, and that's a beautiful thing. Blended families, multicultural traditions, and diverse backgrounds make family life richer, more dynamic, and full of opportunities to learn and grow together. As a grandparent, your role is to embrace this evolving landscape with love, respect, and an open heart. While it may not always be easy to navigate different parenting approaches, new traditions, and changing family structures, being a source of warmth, inclusivity, and support will strengthen your bond with your grandchildren and create lasting memories that celebrate your unique family.

Understanding and respecting different parenting approaches is one of the first steps in successfully grandparenting within a blended or multicultural family. Each parent brings their own experiences, values, and traditions into a child's life, and sometimes these may differ from the way you raised your own children. It can be tempting to step in with advice, but it's important to first listen and observe. If your grandchild's parents have chosen a parenting style that feels unfamiliar to you—whether it's gentle parenting, strict scheduling, or a particular cultural practice—approach it with curiosity rather than judgment. Ask thoughtful questions: "I'd love to learn more about why this is important to you," or "How can I support you in raising the kids in a way that aligns with your values?" This approach fosters respect and keeps communication open, ensuring that your presence remains a positive force in your grandchild's life.

Embracing diversity in family traditions is another wonderful way to create meaningful connections. If your grandchild is part of a multicultural family, take the time to celebrate their heritage. Learn about the holidays they observe, the foods they love, and the customs that are important to them. If they celebrate Lunar New Year, Diwali, Hanukkah, or Día de los Muertos, show enthusiasm and participate! Cooking a traditional dish together, attending a cultural event, or simply asking about the significance of these celebrations sends a powerful message: "Your background matters, and I love that it's part of who you are." At the same time, don't be afraid to share your own traditions. Grandparents serve as a bridge between generations, and blending old and new customs creates a family identity that is both rooted and ever-evolving.

One challenge that sometimes arises in blended families is navigating relationships with multiple sets of grandparents. If your grandchild has multiple step-grandparents, it's important to establish your unique bond without feeling like you have to compete. Love isn't a limited resource, and children benefit from having many adults in their lives who care for them. Instead of comparing relationships, focus on what makes your connection special. Whether it's a particular activity you always do together, a nickname only you use, or a tradition you create just for the two of you, these small but meaningful touches help define your role in their lives.

Step-grandparenting is another unique dynamic that requires patience and an open heart. Becoming a step-grandparent can be an adjustment, especially if the children already have strong bonds with other grandparents. The key is to give the relationship time to develop naturally. Rather than trying to force a connection, focus on simply being present. Engage with them in a way that feels comfortable—whether it's attending their soccer games, asking about their favorite hobbies, or sharing a simple tradition like making pancakes together on Sunday mornings. Avoid using labels like "real" or "step" when talking about family; instead, emphasize love and inclusion. Every child wants to feel accepted, and by welcoming them fully into your heart, you create a relationship that is built on trust rather than obligation.

Creating a warm and inclusive environment for all grandkids, no matter their background, is at the heart of successful grandparenting in a blended or multicultural family. Sometimes, children might feel torn between different parts of their family or unsure about where they belong. Your role is to be the safe space—a place where they never have to question whether they are loved. Simple gestures, like displaying photos of all your grandkids together, remembering important details about their lives, or making an effort to include everyone in family traditions, go a long way in making every child feel seen and valued.

If language differences exist within your blended family, making an effort to learn a few key phrases in another language can show your grandchild how much you care. Whether it's learning how to say "I love you" or "Good job" in their other language, this small effort can have a profound impact. Language is deeply tied to identity, and acknowledging that part of your grandchild's heritage creates a stronger connection.

And of course, a little humor helps in navigating the quirks of blended and multicultural families. Maybe you grew up believing that adding ketchup to eggs was a culinary crime, but your grandchild insists it's the best breakfast ever. Maybe their family dances around the house to music you've never heard before, and they find it hilarious when you attempt the moves. Lean into these moments. Laugh with them. Show them that family isn't about being the same—it's about embracing differences with joy and love.

Another challenge some grandparents face is feeling left out when new traditions replace old ones. Perhaps your grandkids now celebrate a holiday you never observed, or their family dynamic has shifted in a way that makes things feel unfamiliar. Instead of seeing this as a loss, view it as an opportunity to learn and grow. Adaptation doesn't mean forgetting where you come from—it means making room for something new while still cherishing the old. Encourage your grandkids to teach you about their family's traditions, and in turn, share your own. This mutual exchange builds bridges rather than barriers.

At the end of the day, the heart of grandparenting remains unchanged: it's about love, connection, and making your grandkids feel cherished just as they are. Blended families and multicultural backgrounds only add richness to that experience, offering new traditions, new perspectives, and new ways to express love. By being open, supportive, and eager to learn alongside your grandchildren, you reinforce the most important lesson of all— that family, no matter how it's structured, is always built on love.

Chapter 12

Being a Grandparent to a Child with Special Needs

Being a grandparent is a gift, but being a grandparent to a child with special needs is an extraordinary opportunity to offer love, support, and encouragement in ways that can profoundly shape your grandchild's life. Whether your grandchild has autism, Down syndrome, ADHD, a physical disability, or any other unique challenge, your role is one of unconditional love and steady presence. This journey may come with its own set of learning curves, but with patience, an open heart, and a willingness to embrace both the challenges and joys, you can form an unbreakable bond with your grandchild while also providing invaluable support to their parents.

One of the most meaningful ways to be a source of strength in your grandchild's life is by offering support to their parents. Raising a child with special needs can be both rewarding and exhausting, and many parents carry the weight of responsibilities that go beyond traditional parenting. Offering help in practical ways—whether it's providing respite care so they can have a break, assisting with therapy appointments, or simply lending a listening ear—can make a world of difference. Sometimes, the most powerful thing you can say to the parents is, "I see how much you're doing, and you're doing an amazing job." Your validation and encouragement can uplift them in ways they may not always express.

Understanding your grandchild's unique challenges and strengths is essential in deepening your relationship with them. Every child, regardless of their abilities, wants to feel valued for who they are. Taking the time to learn about their diagnosis, their interests, and the ways they communicate and interact with the world allows you to engage with them in meaningful ways. If they respond well to routine, create a special ritual just for the two of you—perhaps reading the same book each time you visit or playing a familiar game. If they struggle with sensory overload, make your home a calming space where they feel safe and comfortable. Recognizing and celebrating their strengths, no matter how big or small, reinforces the idea that they are deeply loved just as they are.

Finding activities that align with their abilities and interests is a beautiful way to strengthen your connection. Some children with special needs thrive in creative activities like painting, music, or storytelling, while others may find joy in structured activities like puzzles or nature walks. If your grandchild enjoys movement, consider activities like swimming, dancing, or even a simple game of catch adapted to their comfort level. Grandparents who take the time to explore what brings their grandchild joy create an environment where they feel encouraged and accepted. The key is to be flexible—what works one day may not work the next, and that's perfectly okay. The most important thing is showing up, being patient, and embracing the moment for what it is.

Patience and encouragement are the cornerstones of grandparenting a child with special needs. There may be moments when communication is difficult, when meltdowns happen, or when progress seems slow—but your steady, loving presence is more powerful than you realize. Every small milestone, from making eye contact to trying a new food, is a victory worth celebrating. Instead of focusing on what a child "should" be doing, celebrate what they are doing. Your words matter—phrases like "I love the way you did that!" or "I'm so proud of you for trying something new" can boost their confidence and reinforce their sense of self-worth.

Humor also has a place in this journey. Sometimes, the best way to handle challenging situations is to find the joy and lightness in them. If your grandchild has a habit of arranging their toys in a very specific way, instead of seeing it as rigid, see it as a sign of their meticulous nature and creative mind. If they repeat the same phrase over and over, join in on the fun and make it a game. Laughter can ease tensions, create bonds, and remind everyone that even in the midst of challenges, there is so much to celebrate.

One of the greatest gifts you can give your grandchild is advocating for their needs while ensuring they feel included in family life. If family gatherings tend to be overwhelming, suggest small adjustments—maybe a quiet space where they can retreat, or a change in routine to make them more comfortable. Educating other family members about their needs and strengths can also foster a more inclusive and understanding environment. The more love and patience a child with special needs receives, the more they thrive.

At the heart of it all, being a grandparent to a child with special needs is about presence—being there, learning, adapting, and loving without condition. Your patience, support, and unwavering love will leave a lasting imprint on their heart. In return, you will experience a bond filled with pure, unfiltered joy and the kind of love that transforms both you and your grandchild. And in the end, isn't that what grandparenting is all about?

Chapter 13

The Role of Grandparents as Caregivers

For many grandparents, the role of caregiver is not just about weekend visits and occasional babysitting—it becomes a full-time responsibility. Whether due to unforeseen circumstances, family challenges, or personal choice, stepping into the role of a primary caregiver for your grandchild can be both incredibly rewarding and deeply demanding. It is a journey filled with love, resilience, and moments of both exhaustion and joy. While it may not have been the path you envisioned, embracing this new chapter with an open heart and a sense of purpose can make it one of the most meaningful experiences of your life.

When grandparents become primary caregivers, the initial adjustment period can be overwhelming. Suddenly, routines shift, and responsibilities expand in ways that might feel reminiscent of your own parenting days—but with a few more gray hairs and a little less energy. There is no manual for stepping back into a parental role after raising your own children, but one of the first and most important steps is to establish a structure that works for both you and your grandchild. Setting routines, ensuring a stable home environment, and making time for both responsibilities and fun can help create a sense of security and normalcy for your grandchild.

Balancing the line between parenting and grandparenting can be tricky. Grandparents are often seen as the ones who indulge and spoil, but when you're the primary caregiver, you must also enforce rules, set boundaries, and handle discipline. This transition can be difficult for both you and your grandchild, especially if they were used to seeing you in a purely "fun" role. The key is consistency—finding a way to maintain the nurturing and warmth that comes naturally while also establishing expectations and stability. It's okay to still have those special grandparent moments, but they must be woven into a daily life that also includes responsibilities and structure.

Managing stress and seeking support is essential. Being a caregiver, especially later in life, comes with physical, emotional, and mental challenges. It is easy to fall into the mindset of putting the child's needs above your own at all times, but burnout is a real concern. Seeking out support—whether from local community groups, online forums for grandparent caregivers, or even professional counseling—can provide valuable resources and reassurance that you are not alone. Accepting help from friends, extended family, or respite programs can give you the breaks you need to recharge. Remember, taking care of yourself is not selfish—it allows you to continue showing up as the best version of yourself for your grandchild.

Despite the challenges, this role can also be deeply fulfilling. Grandparents who raise their grandchildren often develop incredibly strong bonds with them, ones built on trust, shared experiences, and an immense amount of love. The impact you have on their lives will shape their future in ways you may not fully see in the moment. Whether it's helping them with schoolwork, teaching them life skills, or simply being there to comfort them when they're struggling, the influence of a grandparent as a caregiver is immeasurable.

Humor, as always, is a great tool in this journey. There will be moments when you wonder how you are going to keep up, when you find yourself explaining technology you don't understand, or when your grandchild rolls their eyes at your outdated slang. Laugh through it. Find joy in the small, silly moments—whether it's dancing in the kitchen, making pancakes in the shape of animals, or realizing you've been pronouncing a trendy word wrong for months. Laughter can turn exhaustion into fond memories and remind you both that, at the end of the day, love and connection matter more than anything else.

Making this experience positive and fulfilling for both you and your grandchild requires a mindset of adaptability, patience, and appreciation for the unexpected joys that come with raising a child the second time around. It's about embracing the messiness of life, accepting that some days will be harder than others, and remembering that love is the foundation of everything. No matter the circumstances that led you to this role, you are giving your grandchild something invaluable—a stable home, a guiding hand, and the kind of love that only a grandparent can provide.

The journey of being a grandparent caregiver is not always easy, but it is one of profound impact. In the years to come, when your grandchild looks back at their childhood, they will remember not just the meals you cooked or the rules you enforced, but the unwavering love, comfort, and sense of belonging you gave them. And that, above all else, is what makes this journey so incredibly meaningful.

Chapter 14

Teaching Values and Life Lessons

One of the greatest gifts a grandparent can offer a grandchild isn't something that comes wrapped in a bow—it's the wisdom, values, and life lessons passed down through everyday moments. Grandparents play an essential role in shaping character, helping children navigate the complexities of life with kindness, resilience, and compassion. These lessons don't have to be taught in formal sit-down talks. More often than not, they are absorbed through the small, everyday interactions—through the way you speak to others, handle challenges, and show love and patience in the simplest moments.

Passing down kindness, gratitude, and respect begins with modeling these behaviors. Grandchildren learn by watching, and every interaction is an opportunity to demonstrate values that will stay with them for a lifetime. A simple act of holding the door open for a stranger, sincerely thanking a waiter, or greeting neighbors with a warm smile may seem small, but these moments shape a child's understanding of how to treat others. Saying "please" and "thank you" isn't just about politeness; it's about recognizing the humanity in others and appreciating what we have.

A wonderful way to instill gratitude is through storytelling. Grandparents often have rich life experiences that contrast with the fast-paced, convenience-filled world their grandchildren know. Sharing stories about growing up without the internet, cherishing homemade gifts, or making do with what was available helps children appreciate what they have today. It's not about making them feel guilty—it's about helping them see that joy isn't found in material things, but in relationships, experiences, and a sense of purpose. A practical approach is to create a "gratitude jar" together, where each week, you both write down something you're grateful for. Over time, this simple act reinforces the habit of focusing on the positives in life.

Resilience is another invaluable trait that grandparents are uniquely positioned to teach. You have lived through challenges, hardships, and changes that your grandchild hasn't yet faced. Whether it's personal loss, career struggles, or difficult times in history, your perspective can offer them reassurance that obstacles are temporary and that setbacks don't define a person. Teaching resilience isn't about tough love—it's about showing that failure is just a stepping stone. Sharing a time you made a mistake and how you overcame it can be more powerful than any lecture about perseverance. For example, if they feel discouraged after failing a test or losing a game, telling them about a time you faced failure but found a way forward reassures them that setbacks are just part of the journey.

Fostering a growth mindset in children—helping them see challenges as opportunities rather than failures—can be one of the most empowering lessons a grandparent can provide. Encouraging phrases like, "You're still learning," or "I love how you keep trying," reinforce the idea that ability isn't fixed and that persistence leads to progress. When a grandchild struggles with something new, instead of saying, "You're not good at this," try, "You're not good at this yet." A small shift in words can make all the difference in how they approach challenges in life. A great way to reinforce this is to try something new together— perhaps learning a musical instrument, attempting a challenging puzzle, or cooking a difficult recipe.

Demonstrating that you're willing to learn and make mistakes alongside them reinforces the lesson that improvement takes time and effort.

Empathy and compassion are values that seem more important now than ever. Teaching a child to step into another person's shoes can shape their entire outlook on life. Grandparents have the advantage of time—time to sit, to listen, and to nurture emotional intelligence in ways that busy parents may not always have the opportunity to do. Reading books together that explore different perspectives, talking about emotions openly, or even volunteering together can reinforce the idea that kindness isn't just about good manners—it's about making the world a better place. If your grandchild has a conflict with a friend, guiding them through questions like, "How do you think they felt?" or "What could you do to help fix things?" encourages them to develop emotional awareness and problem-solving skills.

Of course, leading by example is the best way to teach any value. If you want your grandchild to show respect, be respectful. If you want them to be compassionate, model compassion in your daily life. This doesn't mean being perfect—it means being mindful. Showing that it's okay to apologize when you make a mistake, to express gratitude sincerely, and to treat others with dignity sends a powerful message that no lecture ever could. Simple gestures like writing a thank-you note together, visiting an elderly neighbor, or donating unused toys can have a lasting impact on their sense of empathy and kindness.

And let's not forget the role of humor in all of this. Teaching life lessons doesn't have to be serious all the time. In fact, some of the best lessons are learned through laughter. Tell them the story of how you once wore mismatched shoes to work because you were in a rush, or how you burned dinner but turned it into a "culinary experiment" instead. Life is full of imperfect moments, and showing them how to laugh through the bumps in the road teaches them resilience in the most lighthearted way.

Another wonderful way to instill values is by creating traditions that reinforce life lessons. Perhaps it's a weekly "kindness challenge" where they perform one small act of kindness and share it with you. Maybe it's an annual "family history night" where you tell them stories about their ancestors, showing them the importance of heritage and resilience. Even something as simple as having a dedicated night for storytelling about mistakes and lessons learned can make a profound impact over time.

At its core, grandparenting is about guiding children not just with words, but with actions and love. The values you pass down—kindness, gratitude, resilience, empathy—will shape how they move through the world long after childhood fades. And years from now, when they're holding the door open for someone, facing a challenge with determination, or simply calling you to say thank you, you'll know that those little lessons, taught in the quiet moments, truly made a difference.

Chapter 15

Creating a Grandparent's Legacy

Grandparents have a special place in a family's story, not just as loving figures in the present, but as the keepers of memories, traditions, and wisdom. Long after the toys and games are forgotten, the love, lessons, and values passed down from a grandparent remain. Creating a grandparent's legacy isn't about wealth or material possessions; it's about the emotional imprint left behind—the moments, stories, and life lessons that continue to shape future generations.

Leaving an emotional legacy begins in the smallest moments. It's in the way you comfort a child after a tough day, in the bedtime stories told again and again, in the warm meals shared at the kitchen table. Children may not remember every single thing you say, but they will remember how you made them feel—safe, loved, and unconditionally cherished. Every conversation, every hug, and every shared experience becomes part of that legacy.

A grandparent's legacy is built not just through spoken words, but through actions. The values you embody—kindness, patience, perseverance, and generosity—are observed and absorbed by your grandchildren. If you treat others with respect and compassion, they will learn to do the same. If you approach life with resilience, they will internalize that strength. If you find joy in the little things, they will learn to do so as well.

One of the most meaningful ways to preserve your legacy is by creating a "Grandparent Journal." This could be a notebook filled with memories, reflections, and personal stories. Imagine your grandchild years from now flipping through handwritten pages, reading about your childhood adventures, your greatest life lessons, and even the silly moments that made you laugh. Writing about how you met their grandparental partner, what the world was like when you were young, or what dreams you had as a child creates a bridge between generations. You don't have to be a professional writer—your love and sincerity will shine through in every word. Some grandparents even choose to record their stories through audio or video messages, ensuring that their voice and laughter remain part of the family forever.

The best gifts a grandparent can give aren't things that can be bought. They are the traditions, rituals, and simple joys that become cherished memories. Maybe it's the way you always make homemade waffles on Sunday mornings, or the fact that you have a secret handshake only you and your grandchild know. Maybe it's a tradition of writing each other letters or creating a time capsule together. These traditions become the glue that binds generations and gives children a deep sense of belonging.

Another way to leave a lasting legacy is through acts of kindness that demonstrate what truly matters in life. Volunteering together, writing letters to those in need, planting a tree in the backyard that will grow as your grandchildren do —these are tangible ways to show that the impact of a good heart is everlasting. Even teaching them how to cook a favorite family recipe turns into something more than just a meal—it becomes a shared experience, a tradition that they will one day pass down.

One way to ensure your love lives on for generations is through storytelling. The stories you tell—about your own grandparents, about the family's history, about challenges and triumphs—

become the fabric of your grandchild's understanding of where they come from. Whether it's tales of resilience, humor, or great adventures, these stories shape their identity. Even better, encourage them to ask questions. "What was your favorite childhood memory?" "What was the hardest thing you ever went through?" "What advice would you give your younger self?" These conversations become a treasure chest of wisdom for them to carry forward.

Legacy isn't just about looking back—it's also about how you inspire the future. Teaching your grandchild values like kindness, perseverance, and gratitude ensures that the lessons you hold dear will live on in them. Encouraging them to pursue their passions, to embrace learning, and to treat others with empathy is a way of shaping their future even when you are no longer physically present. Helping them understand the importance of resilience by sharing stories of your own challenges and triumphs gives them the courage to face their own obstacles with strength and grace.

And let's not forget the importance of humor in all of this. If you're known for your funny stories, your love of silly songs, or the way you always manage to burn at least one dish during the holidays, embrace it. These quirks become part of your legend. Grandkids will tell stories for years about how "Grandpa always danced in the kitchen" or "Grandma had the world's worst sense of direction but never let it stop her from an adventure."

Another deeply meaningful way to ensure your legacy lasts is by creating physical keepsakes that carry sentimental value. Perhaps it's a quilt made from old family clothes, a scrapbook filled with handwritten notes, or a photo album detailing family history. These items become tangible pieces of your love that your grandchildren can hold onto even when you're not around. Many grandparents also choose to write letters to be opened on special occasions—birthdays, graduations, weddings—so their words can continue to guide their grandchild at different stages of life.

At the heart of it all, creating a grandparent's legacy is about love—how deeply you give it, how freely you share it, and how well you make sure your grandkids know they carry that love with them always. The greatest legacy isn't something you leave behind; it's something you leave within them. A legacy built on love, wisdom, laughter, and cherished moments will last far beyond your years and continue to shape generations to come.

Conclusion

As this book comes to a close, the journey of grandparenting continues—one of the most joyful, meaningful, and fulfilling roles life has to offer. Being a grandparent is not just about sharing wisdom or passing down traditions; it's about embracing every moment, big and small, and creating a lasting imprint on the hearts of your grandchildren. Whether you are guiding them through life lessons, offering a warm hug when they need comfort, or simply sitting beside them in quiet companionship, your presence is one of the greatest gifts you can give.

Grandparenting is a privilege, a second chance to witness the wonder of childhood and experience love in its purest form. The laughter of a grandchild, the sparkle in their eyes when they see you, the way they instinctively seek you out for guidance and comfort—these are the priceless rewards of this special role. Every stage of their life presents new opportunities to connect, to teach, and to share moments that will become cherished memories.

One of the most important things to remember is that you don't have to be perfect to be the best grandparent you can be. Your grandchildren don't need you to have all the answers or to follow some grand blueprint for success. What they need is your time, your presence, and your love. They will remember the way you made them feel—safe, special, and unconditionally cherished. They will remember the stories you told, the lessons you taught, and the laughter you shared. And in the moments they face challenges or uncertainties, they will carry your words and your love with them like an invisible safety net.

If there is one call to action in this book, it is this: **be the grandparent you wish you had.** Be the one who listens with patience, who offers encouragement without judgment, and who celebrates their successes as much as you comfort them through their failures. Be the grandparent who makes time, who shows up, who builds traditions, and who makes every child in your life feel like they are the most important person in the world.

Grandparenting is not about age; it's about attitude. It's about embracing new experiences, being willing to learn from your grandchildren as much as they learn from you, and finding joy in the everyday moments. Whether you are near or far, whether you see them daily or only a few times a year, the impact you have on their lives is immeasurable. Love transcends distance, and the connections you build now will echo for generations.

So go forward with confidence, knowing that you are making a difference in the lives of your grandchildren simply by being present, being engaged, and being yourself. Leave them with stories to tell, traditions to continue, and values to carry forward. Show them that love is not measured in grand gestures but in the steady, unwavering presence of someone who cares deeply for them.

And most of all, enjoy every moment. Because grandparenting, with all its laughter, its challenges, its heartwarming surprises, and its deeply rewarding connections, is truly one of life's greatest adventures.

List of content

Made in the USA
Monee, IL
08 April 2025

15374990R00059